Numbers, Symbols, And Matters

Cognate In The Tarot

Frater Achad

Kessinger Publishing's Rare Reprints

Thousands of Scarce and Hard-to-Find Books on These and other Subjects!

- Americana
- Ancient Mysteries
- Animals
- Anthropology
- Architecture
- Arts
- Astrology
- Bibliographies
- Biographies & Memoirs
- Body, Mind & Spirit
- Business & Investing
- Children & Young Adult
- Collectibles
- Comparative Religions
- Crafts & Hobbies
- Earth Sciences
- Education
- Ephemera
- Fiction
- Folklore
- Geography
- Health & Diet
- History
- Hobbies & Leisure
- Humor
- Illustrated Books
- Language & Culture
- Law
- Life Sciences
- Literature
- Medicine & Pharmacy
- Metaphysical
- Music
- Mystery & Crime
- Mythology
- Natural History
- Outdoor & Nature
- Philosophy
- Poetry
- Political Science
- Science
- Psychiatry & Psychology
- Reference
- Religion & Spiritualism
- Rhetoric
- Sacred Books
- Science Fiction
- Science & Technology
- Self-Help
- Social Sciences
- Symbolism
- Theatre & Drama
- Theology
- Travel & Explorations
- War & Military
- Women
- Yoga
- *Plus Much More!*

We kindly invite you to view our catalog list at:
http://www.kessinger.net

CHAPTER EIGHT.

CONCERNING NUMBERS, SYMBOLS AND MATTERS COGNATE.

The Three Interpretations of the Numbers from 1 to 10, given in "The Equinox" Volume I. Number 5, are so brief, concise and clear, that I am fain to depart from my intention to refrain from using books of reference and, with due acknowledgments to Fra. P., quote the passages in full.

I.

0. The Negative—the Infinite—the Circle, or the Point.

1. The Unity—the Positive—the Finite—the Line, derived from 0 by extension. The divine Being.

2. The Dyad—the Superfices, derived from 1 by reflection $\frac{1}{1}$ or by revolution of the line around its end. The Demiurge. The Divine Will.

3. The Triad, the Solid, derived from 1 and 2 by addition. Matter. The divine Intelligence.

4. The Quaternary, the solid existing in Time, matter as we know it. Derived from 2 by multiplication. The Divine Repose.

5. The Quinary, Force or Motion. The inter-

play of the divine Will with matter. Derived from 2 and 3 by addition.

6. The Senary, Mind. Derived from 2 and 3 by multiplication.

7. The Septenary, Desire. Derived from 3 and 4 by addition (There is however a secondary attribution of 7, making it the holiest and most perfect of the numbers).

8. The Ogdoad, Intellect (also Change in Stability). Derived from 2 and 3 by multiplication, $8=2^3$.

9. The Ennead, Stability in Change. Derived from 2 and 3 by multiplication, $9=3^2$.

(Note, all numbers divisible by nine are still so divisible, however the order of the figures is shifted.)

10. The Decad, the divine End. Represents 1 returning to O. Derived from $1+2+3+4$.

11. The Hendecad, the accursed shells, that only exist without the divine Tree. $1+1=2$, in the evil sense of not being 1.

II.

0. The Cosmic Egg.

1. The Self of Deity, beyond Fatherhood and Motherhood.

2. The Father.

3. The Mother.

4. The Father made flesh—authoritative and paternal.

5. The Mother made flesh—fierce and active.

6. The Son—partaking of all these natures.

7. The Mother degraded to mere animal emotion.

8. The Father degraded to mere animal reason.

9. The Son degraded to mere animal life.

10. The Daughter, fallen and touching with her hands the shells.

It will be noticed that this order represents creation as progressive degeneration—which we are compelled to think of as evil. In the human organism the same arrangement will be noticed.

III.

0. The Pleroma of which our individuality is the monad: the "All-Self".

1. The Self—the divine Ego of which man is rarely conscious.

2. The Ego; that which thinks "I"—a falsehood, because to think "I" is to deny "not—I" and thus create the Dyad.

3. The Soul; since 3 reconciles 2 and 1, here are placed the aspirations to divinity. It is also the receptive as 2 is the assertive self.

4—9. The Intellectual Self, with its branches:

    4. Memory.

    5. Will.

    6. Imagination.

    7. Desire.

    8. Reason.

    9. Animal being.

6. The Conscious Self of the Normal Man;

thinking itself free, and really the toy of its surroundings.

9. The Unconscious Self of the Normal Man. Reflex actions, circulation, breathing, digestion, etc., all pertain here.

10. The illusory physical envelope; the scaffolding of the building.

****

The above quotations will give the Student food for thought, and should be carefully studied in the light of what has been written in the previous chapters.

The study of the numbers above Ten involves a great deal of work, and far too lengthy an explanation for this brief treatise. In the SEPHER SEPHIROTH (to be found in "The Equinox" Vol. I, Number 8), we have a more or less complete Qabalistic Dictionary of Numbers and their corresponding Words. This book is quite invaluable. The Student, as time goes on and he advances upon the Path, finds CERTAIN NUMBERS are of peculiar importance to him, and these become so closely associated with his Work, that they form Keys to the innermost recesses of his being. These will not always be the same for each student, rather each must discover his own, sometimes by years of toil. The writer has found the Numbers 0, 1, 13, 31, 86, 93, 111, 136, 141, 165, 300, 418, 419, 496, 620, 777, 913, 963, all very closely associated with his Work,

besides, in a more general way, such great Numbers
as 65, 78, 156, 666, etc.

It is not within the scope of this work to discuss
the many wonderful things that have arisen in connection with the above Numbers, as far as the
author is concerned, but in order to give the Student some idea of the Nature of the Sepher Sepi-
roth, and how words may be connected through
their numerical value, I will take 31 numbers and
their equivalents as an example. The first 24 of
these numbers have been chosen simply on account
of their close juxtaposition on the TREE of LIFE.
The others, being of the Grand Scale, are interesting on that account. I commence with 12, since 1
and 2 are Kether and Chokmah, then 13, as 1 and
3=Kether and Binah, and so on.

12

He longed for, missed	אוה
He departed, went forth	אזד
A little book, pamphlet, letter; tools	גמ
To multiply	דגה
A City of Edom	הבה
HE. (ה Is referred to Mater, ו to Pater, א to Corona)	הוא
Vau; hook, nail, pin	וו
This, that	זה
To penetrate, be sharp; (Ch.) one	חד

13

A small bundle, bunch	אגדה
Beloved. Love	אהבה

Unity אחד

Hated איב

Emptiness בהו

Raised up גהה

Chokmah, 42-fold Name in Yetzirah גי
  (See 777)

Anxiety דאגה

A Fisher דוג

Thunder; to meditate; he removed הגה

A city of Edom הדד

Here; this זו

A locust חגב

He shall come יבא

16

Hyssopus אזוב

He seized, cleaved to אחז

Elevated, exalted, high גבוה

(Verb. subst.) Injury, war, lust; fell הוה

She היא

Alas!—Woe וי

Like, equal to זוג

21

Existence, Being, the Kether-name of אהיה
  GOD

But, yet, certainly אך

Deep meditation הגיג

Ah!—Alas! הוי

Purity, innocence זהו

Vide Sepher Yetzirah יהו

23

Parted, removed, separated   זחח

Joy   חדוה

A thread   חוט

Life   חיה

24

He whom I love   אהובי

He who loves me   אוהבי

A Mercurial GOD. His essence   אבוגה

    is אן, 8

Substance; a body   גויה

A pauper   דך

Angel of 2 C.   הבביה

Abundance   זין

A water-pot, a large earthen vessel   כד

The Numbers of the Sephiroth of the   26

    Middle Pillar; $1 + 6 + 9 + 10$

[Vide K.D. L.C.K. p. 273]   הויה

Seeing, looking at   חוזה

Sight, vision   חזוה

TETRAGRAMMATION, "Jehovah"   יהוה

    the Unutterable Name, the Lost Word

Kebad, husband of the impure Lilith   כבד

    [K.D. L.C.K. 464]

31

How?   איך

GOD of Chesed, and of Kether of Briah   אל

To go   הוך
A beating, striking, collision   הכאה
And there was.   [Vide S.D.I. par. 31]   ויהי
K. of S. Fig. 31   ייאי
Not   לא

                                                                 32

Coalescence of אהיה and יהוה Macrop-   אהיהוה
   rosopus and Microprosopus.   This is
   symbolized by the Hexagram.   Sup-
   pose the 3 ה's conceal the 3 Mothers
   א, מ & ש and we get 358 q. v.
Lord   בל
Angel of 5 W.   והויה
Copula Maritalis   זיווג
Was pure   זכה
Zig-zag, fork-lighting   חזיז
Unity K.D. L.C.K. p. 432   יחיד
Glory   כבוד
Mind, heart   לב

                                                                 35

Agla, a name of GOD; notariqon of   אגלא
   Ateh Gibor le-Olahm Adonai
Boundary limit   גבל
He will go   יהך

                                                                 45

Intelligence of ♄   אגיאל
Adam   אדם

The Fool	אמר
Redemption, liberation	גאולה
To grow warm	חם
Heaven of Tiphareth	זבול
Hesitated. [Vide no. 405]	זחל
Spirit of ♄	זזאל
She who ruins	חבלה
Tet. in Yetzirah	יוד הא ואו הא
Greatly, strongly	מאד
Yetzirah's 'Secret Nature' [Vide I.R.Q. xxxiv.]	מה

46

A name of GOD	אלהי
A female slave; cubitus	אמה
Tin, the metal of ♃	בדיל
A dividing, sundering, separation	הבדלה
Angel of 7 S.	ההאל
A ruiner	חובל
Angel ruling ♉	טואל
Levi, Levite	לוי

47

Foolish, silly. (Stultus)	אויל
A weeping	בכיה
Cloud; high place; waves; fortress	במה
Angel ruling ♍	יואל
To clutch, hold	חלט

54

A basin, bowl, vessel. [Ex. xxiv. 6]	אגן
Rest	דמי
A Tribe of Israel; to judge, rule. [Vide K.D. L.C.K. p. 37]	דן
Pertaining to summer	חֻם
My flame; enchantments	להטי
A bed; stick, rod	מטה
To remove	נד

56

Dread, terror	אימה
He suffered	אנה
Angel of 4 C.	הייאל
Day	יום
Beautiful	נאה

58

[Vide no. 499]	אהבים
[Vide K.D. L.C.K. p. 69] An ear	אזן
Night Demon of 1st Dec. ♪	דאגן
My strength, power, might	חילי
Love, kindness, grace; notariqon of Chokmah Nesethrah, the Secret Wisdom	חן
Ruler of Water	טליהד
Angel of 6 S.	ייזאל
Angel of 3 P.	להחיה
[Vide K.D. L.C.K. p. 69]	נח

67

[Vide K.D. L.C.K. p. 57]   אוני
The Understanding   בינה
Night Demon of 3ʳᵈ Dec. II   וינא
Zayin   זין
Debased   זלל
To embalm   חנט
Angel of 3 C.   יבמיה

69

A manger, stable; an enclosure   אבוס
Myrtle   הדם
L.A. Angel of ♓   וכביאל

There are 78 cards in the Tarot. Σ (1—12).   78
    The Mystic Number of Kether as Hua.
    The sum of the Key-Numbers of the Super-
    nal Beard
Angel of 10 W.   אומאל
Angel of Ra Hoor Khuit   איואס
Briatic Palace of Chesed   היכל אהבה
Angel of ♂   זמאל
The breaker, dream   חלם
To pity   חמל
To initiate   חנך
Angel of 2 S.   יזלאל
Angel of 1ˢᵗ Dec. ♉   כדמדי
Bread (P's. lxxviii. 25)=חלם,   לחם
    by metathesis. [K.D. L.C.K. p. 500]

Angel of 2 S. מבהאל
The Influence from Kether מזלא
Salt מלח
The name of a Giant עזא

79

Boaz, one of the Pillars of the Temple בעז
  of Solomon
Die גוע
Angel of 8 S. ומבאל
Jachin, one of the Pillars of the Temple יאחין
  of Solomon
3rd שׁ סיט
Conjunction, meeting, union עדה

87

[Vide K.D. L.C.K. p. 114] אלון
A cup אסוך
Angel of 1st Dec. ♓ בהלמי
Blasphemed גדף
Standards, military ensigns דגלים
Determined זמם
White Storks חסידה
Whiteness; frankincense; Sphere of ☾ לבנה

89

Shut up גוף
Body גוף
Silence דממה
Angel of 9 S. מחיאל

Σ (1—13). The Mystic Number of Kether as   91
　　　Achad.　The Number of Paths in the
　　　Supernal Beard; according to the number
　　　of the Letters, כ=11, etc.

A tree	אילן
Amen.　[Cf 741]	אמן
The Ephod	אפוד
The "יהוה אדני", interlaced	יאהדונהי
Angel of 4 S.	כליאל
Archangel of Geburah	כמאל
Food, fare	מאכל
Angel	מלאך
Daughter, virgin, bride, Kore	מלכא
Manna	מנא
A hut, tent	סוכה
Pekht, 'extension'	פאהה

111

Red.　[Vide Gen. xxv. 25]	אדמונא
A name of GOD	אחד הוא אלהים
A thousand; Aleph	אלף
Ruin, destruction, sudden death	אסן
AUM	אעם
Thick darkness	אפל
Passwords of	יוד יהוה אדני
Mad	מהולל
Angel of ☉	נכיאל
Common holocaust; an ascent	עולה
A Duke of Edom	עלוה
Title of Kether.　(Mirum occultum)	פלא

222

Urias	אוריה
"Unto the Place." [Ex. xxiii. 20]	אל המקום
Whiteness	הוורה
Goodly mountain. [Ex. iii. 25]	הר טוב
Now, already; K'bar, "the river Khebar"; Day Demon of 3rd Dec.	כבר
I will chase	ראויה

333

Qabalah of the Nine Chambers	איק בכר
Choronzon. [Vide Dr Dee, & Lib. 418, 10th Aire]	חורונזון
Snow	שלג

444

The Sanctuary	מקדש
Damascus	דמשק

555

Obscurity	עפתה

666

Σ (1—36). ⊙. The Number of THE BEAST.	
Aleister E. Crowley	אליהיסמהר ה כרעולהי
Aleister Crowley [Rabbi Battiscomber Gunn's v.l.]	אליסטיר קרולי
The number 5, which is 6 (הא), on the Grand Scale	הא x אלף

Qliphoth of ♓   נשימירון

Spirit of ☉   סורת

Ommo Satan, the 'Evil Triad' of
  Satan-Typhon, Apophras, and Besz עממו סתן

The Name Jesus   שם יהשוה

777

The Flaming Sword, if the path from Binah
  to Chesed be taken as = 3. For ג connects
Arikh Anpin with Zauir Anpin.

One is the Ruach of the
  Elohim of Lives   אחת רוח אלהים חיים

The World of Shells   עולם הקליפות

The foregoing will give the Student some little
material to work upon, and to experiment with, in
tracing out some of the correspondences for him-
self, though he needs "The Sepher Sephiroth" for
reference and further research. Also he will find
"The Essay on Number" in "The Temple of Solomon the King," Equinox Vol. I, Number 5, and
"A Note on Genesis," Equinox Volume I, Number
2, of tremendous help and value.

We may now give an example of the way in
which we may use the TAROT SYMBOLS for the
interpretation of certain WORDS. The relation of
these Symbols to the Letters of the Hebrew Alph-
abet, each spelt in full, has been ably shown in one
of the articles mentioned above, but I do not know
that any attempt has been made to interpret the

Names of the 10 Sephiroth in a similar manner. The Symbolism of the Tarot Trumps being Universal, many interpretations could be given representing different planes. Here is one, which came to me yesterday, which if deeply MEDITATED upon, may prove illuminating.

AN ATTEMPT TO INTERPRET THE NAMES OF THE SEPHIROTH FROM MALKUTH TO KETHER BY TAROT. Fra.·. א June 12, 1922, E. V.

10. Malkuth. מלכות· The REDEEMER of the BALANCE of the FORCES OF LIFE is the HIEROPHANT of the UNIVERSE.

9. Yesod. יסוד· The SECRET of TEMPERANCE shown by the HIEROPHANT to the EMPRESS.

8. Hod. הוד· The EMPEROR through the HIEROPHANT finds LOVE (The Empress).

7. Netzach. נצח· Transformation through DEATH awaits the STAR in the CHARIOT.

6. Tiphereth. תפארת· The U N I V E R S A L TOWER is Blasted by the FOLLY of the SUN of the UNIVERSE.

5. Geburah. גבורה· The HOLY LAW of MAGICK as taught by the HIEROPHANT of the SUN is applied by the EMPEROR.

4. Chesed.   חסד· The CHARIOT of TEM-
PERATE-LOVE.

3. Binah.   בינה· The MAGICAL SECRET
of DEATH transforms the EM-
PEROR.

2. Chokmah.   חכמה· The CHARIOT (or Bal-
anced Control) of the LIFE
FORCES, REDEEMS the EM-
PEROR.

1. Kether.   כתר· In the "Hollow of the
Hand" (כ) of the LORD OF
THE FORCES OF LIFE is the
UNIVERSAL SUN.

The Student should take his Tarot Cards and
study them very carefully in connection with the
above, and it may be well if he try to obtain other
interpretations, say in the order from Kether to
Malkuth, representing the Descent of the Light
from above.

He should also study the Shape and Parts of the
"Tree of Life" itself, and he will notice that the
whole forms an ANKH or Egyptian Key of Life,
which is again the symbol of Venus (♀). It should
be noticed how the "Tree" forms Three Pillars,
those of Mercy and Severity, with the Pillar of
Mildness between them. Again, the Hexagram is
formed by the Upper Six Sephiroth, and the lines
of the Pentagram may be drawn by connecting the
upper Five. The "Tree" can be divided into Seven

Planes, etc., etc. In fact, one cannot exhaust the possibilities of its study.

I should like to remark once again, however, that this is, after all, just a CONVENIENT MEANS OF CLASSIFICATION. Sometimes we desire to Symbolize ALL as Unity, and we should probably use merely a Circle or Point. Again, there is the DUAL Aspect. Then the Great THREE-FOLD DIVISION as the TRINITY. Then the FOUR-FOLD nature of the ELEMENTS can be expressed as a SQUARE or CROSS. But once we use the CROSS, there is the POINT OF INTERSECTION indicating the Hidden SPIRIT, so we adopt the Great FIVE-FOLD classification of THE PENTAGRAM, Symbol of THE MICROCOSM, MAN. Again we wish to symbolize our correspondence to the MACRO-COSM and we use the HEXAGRAM, or SIX-FOLD STAR, upon which we place the Planetary Symbols and the Holy Seven-fold Name ARARI-TA, for this Star has a CENTRE which is attributed to The SUN and this makes it also a SEVEN-FOLD means of classification. Next comes our TEN-FOLD QABALISTIC TREE of LIFE, with all its possibilities of extension through the 22 paths, 4 Worlds, etc. and its TAROT ATTRIBU-TIONS. These, again, can just as well be expressed in the form of a Great Wheel, with the TWELVE SIGNS of the ZODIAC on its rim, and it is from the Rulers of the Decanates that the Divinatory meanings of the Small Cards are obtained. Lastly,

since this Wheel has a CENTRE it expresses
THIRTEEN, and we may arrange our Zodiacal
attributions on a GREEK CROSS of THIRTEEN
SQUARES with SPIRIT at the CENTRE. So, you
see, you must not think the Plans are fixed, they
can always be interchanged, according to the
Nature of that aspect we most desire to make promi-
nent.

But remember, in all this diversity, is the One
underlying UNITY, which itself arose from that
which is NOT.

This is the end of this publication.

Any remaining blank pages are for our book binding requirements and are blank on purpose.

To search thousands of interesting publications like this one, please remember to visit our website at:

http://www.kessinger.net

9 781168 644039